Jersey Girl

POETRY BY NORMA PAUL

Lime Press

Jersey Girl
Poetry by Norma Paul

This book is written to provide information and motivation to readers. Its purpose is not to render any type of psychological, legal, or professional advice of any kind. The content is the sole opinion and expression of the author, and not necessarily that of the publisher.

Copyright © 2021 by **Norma Paul**

Artwork by Lee Bourdot

First Published, 2021
Printed in the United States of America.
ISBN: 978-1-954304-83-3 (Ebook)
ISBN: 978-1-954304-84-0 (Paperback)
ISBN: 978-1-954304-85-7 (Hardback)

Published by Lime Press LLC
425 West Washington Street
Suffolk VA, 23434 Suite 4
https://www.lime-press.com/

Pacific Book Review

It is often said that poetry is the language of not only love, but life itself. A language of emotions, or for some the language to help articulate or even escape feelings. For others poetry can be a means of writing about one's life without fully delving into the non-fiction, memoir-style storytelling aspect of things. It stirs the reader's imagination and often elicits imagery and one's deepest emotions, both good and bad.

In author and poet Norma Paul's *Jersey Girl*, the writer articulates several aspects of life in a collection of poetry. Tackling subjects which range from how to go about writing poetry for the youthful, to how the various seasons look, and impact the author from her New Jersey home and even the 2020 Crisis. One of the first things which speaks to the reader when delving into this book is the almost cinematic quality to the narrative. Each poem is unique in its approach and delivery, and the author does an amazing job of engaging the reader on a personal level. The imagery was felt deeply within this book as each poem does an excellent job of painting a picture of the author's life so the readers feels as if they are within the scene.

This is the perfect read for those who enjoy poetry, especially those dealing with a wide range of themes and topics and add a touch of non-fiction, memoir-style storytelling. As a fan of beautiful poetry such as this, it was easy to get lost in the author and poet's story and the lessons and memories they earned along the way, a sentiment many of us can relate to.

A heartfelt, soul-searching and memorable read, author Norma Paul's *Jersey Girl* is a fun and engaging book of poetry. The author does a remarkable job of crafting a powerful and stunning deep dive into creativity and an emotional tapestry that many readers can relate to. If you haven't yet, be sure to grab yourself a copy of this incredible read today!

Dedication

This book is dedicated to the following:

JESSE

TRAVIS

DAKOTA

EUGENE

GARRETT

*FAITH

LUCAS

PERSEPHONE

JORDAN

*In memoriam

Table of Contents

I

The Author

JERSEY GIRL

She may have been born here—
Making her a true Jersey girl—
Or she may have moved to Hillside
As a new teenager
Who quickly learned to sing
"Three cheers for old Hillside High—
Send the freshmen out for gin
And don't let a sober sophomore in."
Which made her a real Jersey girl by proxy.

In any case, if she relishes the taste of
Hard rolls with butter
Taylor ham
Pizza topped with pepperoni
White Castle sliders
Coffee
She can be defined as a Jersey Girl
Which means she always stands up for herself
And her beliefs.

She may never join a political party but
She will vote in every election
Beginning with the high school prom queen who
Led the fight against the denial of attendance by
A gay couple.

When she marries—If she marries—
You can always drop by without the need to
Call her first.
She will not apologize for the mess
Her kids left around.
Not *just* a Jersey girl but a Jersey mom.

Self-reliant, she got a job as soon as her schooling ended.
She does not expect anyone else to support her.
But I will, always, and I believe you would too.

II

Learning to Write

MINING FOR TREASURE

Beauty has never been skin-deep only.
Sunbeams are absorbed within,
flooding their warmth through every fiber,
knowing a storm may pierce the morrow.

I dig into each copper canyon
beneath the verse before my eyes.
My pick-axe scratches each lower level
I descend.

Brilliance is revealed but
oh! it slips from my grasp when I
hold my breath. Silver and gold
await revealing. Poets of old
secrete their source.

I bend to pry beneath each lode
deep in the shaft my spade reveals.

ODYSSEY

Just like a sigh no one else can hear,
Like a secret meant for just one ear
Just like a verse drizzled down in rain
Or did you imagine it bloomed in my brain?

Opening lines looking so unkempt
Speak of hours fruitlessly spent,
Hours lost searching for words to implore.
Did you ever think you could create more?

Your style and your word count shine for some
A charming outlook, tossed like a crumb
To others an abstract thesaurus phrase.
Still you struggle to win some praise.

Published poets stride down the boardwalk blazing.
Turn from their parade although it's amazing.
A few poets find redemption in your heart
But you pick at their provenance from the start.

Stanzas devised speed from one to another
In a feminine way, not like a brother.
Our knowledge is stifled by lack of means
But somehow we plan to emerge as queens.

At last we believe we've hit our stride
Ready to hitch a fantasy ride.
We forge ahead toward our fruitful goal
To turn hollow verses into Odyssey's soul.

"THE CHEW"

It's one pm and on TV three cooks are demonstrating
tricks of their trade while I try to absorb a bit of
what they're sharing with one eye
in the midst of poetic pen to paper.

One Girl Scout Tagalong after another makes its way
into my mouth. I suck off the chocolate coating before
biting into the crispy layer, as a room temperature
roasting chicken is patted dry before being buttered all over.

Inspiration continues to escape my pondering mind
while the dog barks another plea to come in from the cold.
Tagalongs back in the box, I rise to oblige and note that
each new dish demands a squirt of lemon juice.

Clearly it's time to tabulate
the number of words chosen and
how many verses they entail.
One pm has come and gone.

QUEST

From the closing nights of winter to the opening morns of
spring
how long have I pondered the beginning of my muse,
who it is who answered my open inquiring soul,
agitated now with this fruitless search.
I gaze out the window with blue and white above
as if there's the answer, but no words insinuate
their presence. My glance is interrupted by
the orchids on the sill as white overlapping petals
surround their purple eyes. Distraction reigns.
Across the way a mourning dove rides down a swift
descending breeze
while the newly arrived red breast pushes his way upward,
his wet feet dripping morning's dew beneath his flight.

Turning then, I ponder memory to latch onto yesteryear's
sandy beach
when first my pen splashed through inspiration washing in
with the tide.
Who whispered into my beachcombing ear until I felt
compelled to spell it out?
But that was then. Seaweed's buried those ancient rhymes.

Here I sit in a room of my own and contemplate familiar
sweet surrounds that touch each living moment.

Jak stretches his shaggy canine presence across the
armchair of his choice
ever alert to howl when the fire whistle sounds. On the
bookcase,
long stems of a spider plant stretch up and down to one
side
and the other. The art work on the walls, crayoned and
painted by
granddaughters, fills my eyes with color and gratitude.
Pop's handmade chest holds a Mother's Day bouquet
set upon a grandmother's braided pad. I'm convinced
Calliope has not traveled from the Hellenistic Age to
furnish my muse, homespun as it remains.

ANALYSIS

Between the moment when I pick up my pen and the
moment it touches down on the page of my journal,
a sudden realization reveals this is the true beginning
of a telling development in my life's journey.

I hesitate, cock my head to listen. Some unknown voice
whispers to me, guides my fingers to grasp hold of this
stunning knowledge. I am not alone in my search
to reveal meaningful truth.

Beyond my groping to uncover Life's mysteries,
I listen to a robin's staccato rendering of his
mournful melody within my inner being.
It spreads its minor key across my symphonic staff.

Taking a deep breath, I sigh slowly,
reel in my escaping thoughts,
press them together to form
one well-bonded analysis.

READY TO MAKE A NEW BEGINNING

But nothing ever ends.
In the middle of wherever I am,
The past I plot to escape
Will find itself trounced underfoot.
Our lives are woven of many threads,
One strand interwound with another
For strength and permanence.
In today's demands for instant success
No room for failure is tolerated.
A "bride's biscuits" are never experienced
Since perfection is at hand at the corner bakery.

Even the most intimate of marital closeness is
Tried on beforehand. To learn as you go
Induces smug intolerance among peers.
Decades have gone by since anything bridal
Held a bouquet of familiarity for me.
This New Year's Resolution, then, involves no one else,
No one to please, or satisfy, or impress.
Simply put, I plan to reach a deeper self
Beneath casual layers of sensibility
Wrapped around my personhood.
I have an idea it's dark down there.

TUESDAY MORNING

Waiting for enough time to pass
until I can head out the door to
meet the girls at Sweet Jenny's,
I flip through the pages of
Billy Collins' <u>Aimless Love</u> to stop
only at those poems which say
everything they have to say on
just one page. I can't wrap
my poetic mind around more words
than begin and end in just
that short a space.
Believe me, if I craved solutions to
mental mysteries, I would plod on and
glance across to the facing page.
But that would take an amount of
effort which eludes me this morning.
So I pause briefly at Billy's
"In the Evening" to picture
drooping roses and one lone white cat.
Somehow I know they will stay
on my mind until this day ends.

THIS IS JUST TO SAY

This is just to say
I have torn up those last three verses
You wanted me to critique
Knowing you were longing for my
Input
Waiting with bated breath
For my applause.
They were tasty and
Worthy of repetition.
Forgive my destruction.

III

Youth

MANHOOD

Let me stand between the sails,
bare feet against a wooden deck,
facing into the pressing wind
to welcome its bracing challenge.

I take lines in hand to direct
my chosen route, ready to explore
the moving current into each cove
edging the bay.

I stand alone,
without a map, without a mate,
eager to embrace the unknown
lying just around the bend.

Inhaling deep breaths of sea air
as it reveals itself,
I sail on and on
toward tomorrow.

A PRESENCE

At fourteen, the boy is solemn
with searching eyes,
a tremulous mouth,
husky voice
just shy of a whisper.
When he enters a room
inhabited in the main
by imposing adults,
he shrinks into himself,
belying the long limbed
stretch of possibility
tomorrow will decree.
Fueled by overwhelming takes
on daily bread and energy,
he pounces without
hesitation, then brakes in
sudden loss of purpose,
a cloud descending
from his brow. In
certain recognition of the
alien space he occupies,
he turns again and leaves
the interrupted conversation.

IV

Love and Marriage

SONNET

As I recall again that summer's day

We lay beneath the trees within a glen,

Remembrance of your fingering the length of hair

I flung with a shake of my flaxen locks

Recalls the wonder of our feelings' strength, intense,

That carried off our prior playful schemes

As if love's existence between us

Began just then. No memory of former

Hearts' desires materialized along

The quivering stream beside the glen.

You stroked my hair, and a handful of summers away

Your gentle touch played lightly with its

Shift from gold to silver, as if to say

A year's as fleeting as a breathless day.

NEW LIFE

Where white sand ends,
Green grass carpets
The verdant coast as
Light filters through one
Very old spreading Hemlock
Festooned with
Spanish moss.
There blossoms dance in
Afternoon sun.
Within the moss
A cardinal of
Bright repute
Settles into her nest to
Await the dropping of
Her egg, the only birth
Allowed our winged friends.
Come lie with me to sip my wine.
The bottle's cold. We have all day.
We'll celebrate with Mama Bird
Her offspring's descent.

SIDE BY SIDE

Our autumn of accomplishment
pivoted to a winter of discontent.
The days grew dark, and in their spell
I withheld my longing in its shell.
That need to run barefoot down the beach
was faltered by bitter cold.
With arms extended in a fervent reach
my heart retreated from moves too bold.

Each morning I awakened with another plan
to begin again as we had before.
Nothing was changed in our daily span
but the itching need to run out the door.
I could not pinpoint where it all began.
Arguments never made any sense.
One weeping woman, one muted man
were all that remained of the evidence.

Somehow we held on when day was done
to await the rising of the silver moon.
Somehow we returned to where we'd begun.
Thank God, we breathed, it was none too soon.

BLUE SHADOW

Alone at the bay my shadow precedes me
visibly blue as that dot in the sky.
Verdant thoughts swim on before me.
I measure the boards as in days gone by.

His memory lies obscure as my shadow,
always ahead, just clear of my reach,
to paralyze dreams of moving beyond him
free of his hold on this windswept beach.

I bend with the breeze like the gulls
above me, pine to be supple as *their* wings allow.
Abandoned, shadow denies the pavilion.
Darkness/peace envelop me now.

SO CLOSE SO FAR

From 117 Reese Avenue
it's two long blocks to the boardwalk
where nightly meanderings take me
each October evening to
dovetail a search for autumnal
fulfillment with a quest for meaning
in which to enfold my seeking self.

The beach stretches the length of a block
to the first ripple of low tide.
Few oceanfront homes emit light,
stand in wait for another summer.
I feel my summer's heated joy trail
behind me, pinpointing my penchant
for solitude, here beneath Venus.

THE DAY I WATCHED YOU WALK AWAY

The day I watched you walk away
rain came down on London town.
In a Brooklyn sandlot
Pete and Jackie tossed a ball
waiting for the rest of the gang.
Six year old Alice in Ashtabula
finally managed to tie her shoelace.
Yellow school buses made their rounds.
Bells rang between each class.
Doors of department stores reopened.
High heeled shoppers hurried in.
Uptown and downtown subways
spilled their riders into the streets.
Brief cases carried by harried business men
filled office elevators.
Fresh made coffee's odor permeated hallways.
Trade continued. School went on.
Traffic never stood still.
Nothing changed for Pete, or Jackie, or students,
or high heeled shoppers, or business men
or London's rain
the day I watched you walk away.

RULE OF THUMB

First comes love
the story goes
and I concede
everyone knows
to follow the rules
will help it last
but often I wonder
if we can get past
the do's and don'ts
of made for each other
and still survive our
exclusive one another.

You are you and never change
while I try forever to rearrange
my hair, my being,
my inner demeanor
to keep you intrigued
through summer, through winter.
Give it a go, I secretly vow,
flirt and wink and still somehow
come back to the center
of what we deem dear.
Hold me fast. Never fear.

WORTH THE WORK

Looking back, she strives to recover
long-lost strength of work which defines her,
tries to remember nights she would shiver
longing for a promised forever.

He reaches into memory's bank
to bring forth reasons the vision began.
Nights of pain, of sweat, of struggle
culminate in emergence of a man.

Like crumbling rocks in a summer landslide,
one day dissolves into another,
pile up in anthills of might-have-been
as they stumble around each other.

Now one precious, sparkling stone,
the brightest object she possesses,
holds her steadfast with its value
long beyond their daily stresses.

Staggering now in attempts to stand
free and apart from daily grinds,
they meet toe to toe, declare a truce,
invoke a meeting of the minds.

Test it now in solemn wonder.
Hold your breath. Whisper low:
Was it worth the work? They ponder.
Two for one renews their vow.

A STRING OF PEARLS

One joyful day he gifted me
the perfect anniversary,
each bauble round and smooth and white
to grace my throat that very night.
We danced romantic hours away
until the dawn of a brand new day.
That lovely morning in early spring
linked life to love by a treasured string.

Another year flew by before
we reached for the pearls in their hidden drawer
to float once more around the town
in his three-piece suit and my ballroom gown.
Alas and alack how could I find
the knotted string had begun to unwind.
I began to bawl like a little girl
when I found my necklace missing a pearl.

I started to wonder how on earth
one lost jewel could lessen its worth,
hunted through the drawer of the little hutch
in hopes that the gem I'd be able to clutch.
An hour spent searching in my mania
left me feeling quite insania.
Years have gone by. Just as I feared
that elusive pearl simply disappeared.

SEPTEMBER'S STONE

In ancient days, hands of destiny
flung myriads of gems
across the atmosphere
to land by Fate on its month of choice.

In just such a way, glassy diamond peaked in April,
milky pearl in June, while sapphire in all its shades of blue
descended as if appointed by Heaven
on the privileged days of September.

Here lie the deepest hues which originate in
oceans beneath, in skies above,
ranging from soft innocence to burning purple, to
accompany Virgo's perfection, purity.

I enfold a sapphire within my palm,
dwell on its timelessness.

ADRIFT

How long, how long we lie adrift
among golden grasses of yesteryear,
bring back dreams of foreign destinies,
a longing to taste alien treats
luring beyond reach,
enticing blazing tongues,
chilling summer's
appetite for seduction.

Beside your strong, celestial form
I tremble in assailing winds,
recalling what might have been,
a dream fulfilled beneath distant stars,
tender, then, at once complete and
held at bay. Count the days
left behind, the hours to come.
Remembrance remains real.

KAYAK HORSESHOE BEND

Down below Horseshoe Bend on the mighty
Colorado River through Glen Canyon,
I gaze skyward toward canyon walls a
thousand feet above. Here the emerald span,
all flat water with no rapids,
wraps itself around soaring red rock cliffs
fringed by greenery along the banks.

Above, a soft slant of sun peers in.
Staring down into the river depths,
I feel my personhood disappear. Here alone,
a soothing stillness envelops me.
Slivers of sandbars invite a stop but the
unhurried pace set by the Colorado
satisfies my idyllic expedition.

MARITAL DISCORD

In my nudenik phase, I tried
to convince my one and only
to flee with me to a beckoning beach
where we could lay aside
encumbrances of our hostile urbanity.

Over and over I pleaded.
Over and over he declined.

Through the years from then til now,
I learned to respect his diplomacy
but once in a while I long
for lost days of
golden ecstasy.

VILLANELLE

Sipping my Beaujolais, I close each eye
to worldly care and the darkening day,
swallow slowly, soothe worries pressing nigh.

A cloud descends from higher in the sky
until the last bit of sunshine slips away.
Sipping my Beaujolais, I close each eye.

Darkness descends closer while I sigh
for some relief from descending gray,
swallow slowly, soothe worries pressing nigh.

I long for new leaves on the Maple high
to promise Spring again is on its way.
Sipping my Beaujolais, I close each eye.

So like a dream, this day filters by,
a bit like figures in a shadow play.
Swallow slowly, soothe worries pressing nigh.

Reveal honest daylight now. Do not lie.
I'm longing for the best of time to stay.
Sipping my Beaujolais, I close each eye,
swallow slowly, soothe worries pressing nigh.

V

Seasons

BROKEN PROMISE

In nearly the exact center of
my would-be March lawn
one single white crocus
appears on the morning of
early March tenth.
Much against his normal behavior
the naturally curious dog
does not investigate.
The one bright spot remains
all night and all the next morning
until I notice that now there are
two blossoms.

I rack my brain for the memory
of when that bulb had been set into
the earth beneath it
but could not recall ever doing that.
So I accept our Maker's gift to
show me, Yes, Spring is coming,
on its way once more.

Delighted, I ransack my wintry wardrobe
for a fitting, light outfit to brighten my day,
pack away three heavy sweaters,

move boots to the back of the closet,
set the clock for daylight-saving time,
crawl into bed under one fleecy blanket
to anticipate a stroll in a warming breeze.

Alas, it's an icy downpour awaking me now,
as once again, I find a promise unfulfilled.
What happened this time, I wonder.
What have I done to turn my Karma
upside down? I reach for the quilt I let
fall to the floor, snuggle into another
postponement of my plans of
celebration.

APRIL MORN

Late April it was a Tuesday
when through the open window
wakeup call of robins' singing early
early not even five yet
coaxed me out of bed to shut off the radio
so I could hear them better.
It was WYRS, the Christian radio station the birds were
responding to,
voices I leave on all night, going from assorted bits of
philosophy
to a range of melodious expressions,
from Southern Gospel to moving guitars and harps,
strumming across my awareness and unawareness
through dreams and sinking into oblivion and stirring
back and forth through the long hours' stillness.
Once the hymns were stilled, the birds' trilling stopped,
then in hesitation started again—
then trailed off and away.

APRIL EVENING

We lost the sunset when we moved to this side of the bay
but once in a while
this new April evening, say,
it spreads its roseate glow all across the heavens
to touch me here on our grey piece of earth
promising reunion
reminding me of
how many sunsets we parked to watch
no words needed
no hand-holding, no kiss
basking in its suffusion
waiting for our longed for togetherness
to finally come to pass
then stayed with us day after day after year after year
melded us into each other's aspect
held us up through stressed early times of growing into
Oneness
through struggles to find our own footholds
independent of each other's needs.
Again tonight all is remembrance when the
setting sun streams into my aloneness
here
on this side of the Barnegat.

CANOE CANOE?

When we reached Deep River
that bright morning in June
it was amazing how puffy white clouds
spilling like sugar out of skipper blue sky
were reflected in total in the mirror below.

I stared down into space,
began falling out of the canoe
into a grasping sky above. I felt
no waves as I descended the world of water,
my tee shirt plastered to my body.

Eyes opened wide in disbelief, I crawled
beside waving spires of pea-green water lilies
staking their claim on the river's mud.
Polliwogs darted among the stems.
I reached for one, then another.

I could not close my palm against any. They
swam across my face, behind each ear.
I turned this way, then that to no avail.
Bracing bare feet against the clay floor below
I shot up into daylight once again.

Pulling myself back into the canoe,
I sputtered, trying to tell everyone what
I had seen, what I had felt, what I had
lived.
They simply stared.

SUMMER VISION

Coaxing me from fitful sleep
soft across midnight blue
lightning beams played far and wide.

Fireflies danced through foliage of
ancient mulberry trees.

I lingered at my window
inhaling beauty while awaiting
drums of thunder to replace
its sylvan silence.

Quiet remained.
My breath escaped.

--How long had I been
holding it?

SEPTEMBER RAIN

September rain sidles in aslant a sibilant west wind,
drills its relentless tattoo into the seamless fabric
of an autumn afternoon. From the front porch to the
vine-covered gate, florid chrysanthemums flaunt
their homecoming array—pumpkin, gold, cerise,
lift their thirsting palates to a crystalline draft.
drink in the final goodbye kiss of one last
lonely bee.

September rain lingers on the brow,
the mouth, the chin, falls in lazy rivulets
from gabled peaks to garden paths. At dusk
September rain whispers "remember."
Remember the sound of sighs.
Remember the kiss of lonely.
Remember the longing of linger.
September rain slides with ease into one moist
Nocturnal farewell.

AFTER THE RAIN

I slip into the garden, kneel on moist earth,
finger handfuls of seeds, contemplate
life's transitions.
Solace layers itself across
my morning's rising mood.
Inner spirit lifts.

I stand to step among descending bluejays
as they coast into dew-sparkled vines,
light between greening plants.
Wonder fills my being.
A sense of purpose plants itself,
second nature, within.

LEFTOVERS

The Nor'easter came and went as promised
but at the foot of my driveway, puddles gleam
with reflections of the towering Cedar
as if in a mirror. I seem
to recall we viewed the coming storm as twaddle
nothing to fear from the three-day siege
until it grew beyond our expectation
filling its path with eminence. I besiege
my neighbors to recall its rampant fury,
mark the date on your calendar in relief
that the Cedar still stands, with jays now merry
no reason to look back with grief.
It left us close to each other, neighborly,
ready to count on one another, you and me.
Like hands raised in a hail-well salute
our trees gravitate toward winds from the sea.

AFTER SNOW

After snow—after play in frigid temps—
Round and round and round he goes
Pushing the big pink towel with his forelegs
Until he gets it just right to push his chin on
To curl around himself after a long hour
Out on the snow covered yard—after
Scratching at the door he had slammed into
So hard I couldn't open it from inside.
Jak! I called at the back door—
Then whistled again and again—
Beeped the horn of my buried car in the driveway
Thinking he'd run back to investigate that
At least. Nothing worked. Finally phoned
A grandson up the road to come over in his boots
And lead him from the front door, let him in
The back. Jak gulped his dinner,
Flopped down in the living room,
Grateful for his long-sought rescue.

MY FACE CATCHES THE WIND

My face catches the wind
in the glow of myth and morning.
Bright blue embraces my being
as I stretch up in yearning
toward fulfillment of this quest
for truth among the legends
that invade my searching journey
toward redemption of each morrow.

In the glow of myth I ponder
each beginning and each message
meant to clarify the longing
for a morning to discover
yet another heartfelt answer to
an ancient probing mystery
scratching at the surface of my
consciousness and caring.

Bright blue envelops my being.
I surrender to the wind.

SPLINTERED CEDARS

Shaken by breaking thunder,
cedars of Lebanon flake off
their falling shoots, discard aging limbs
in favor of young new growth,

again to dance in the wind,
challenge flames of youth,
apart and away from maturity,
encroaching in the distance.

Divided by bands of genealogy,
splintered segments skip
back in time to prance about,
wild, ageless.

VI

COVID-19 AFTERNOON

Fifteen minute trading halt
All time record losses
Wash your hands.
Pantry open at SPCA
Wash your hands frequently
Supplemental spending bill
Making sure our first responders
have everything they need.
Wash your hands.
Navigating your health
Err on the side of caution
Wash your hands.
If we under-react it could cost us
suppressed immune system.
Wash your hands.
No large gatherings
Relays cancelled.
Feeling uncertain, even anxious
Wash your hands.
Important to balance that
with stress reduction.
Presidential debate between two men

No audience
Avoid gathering in groups of ten or more
Take-out service only.
Wash your hands.
Halt all non-essential business activities
Live day to day.
We do not make these changes lightly.
Happy hours all cancelled.
Mobile testing sites not equipped for the masses.
Developing grant and loan programs.
Working from home.
Wash your hands.

VIRAL LOVERS

Pardon me while I walk
on the other side of the street.
Keep your mask on when we talk.
Our friendship must be kept discreet.
One of these days--
I hope it's soon--
the doctor will give us a shot.
Then we can kiss beneath the moon
as long as your temperature's not too hot.

AN ABERRATION OF RICHES

Immunity enfolds me,
incredible as it seems.
This yawning wilderness,
once an unconditional challenge,
frees my being from the infusion
of Covid culture wars
waged by a neighbor's resistance
to incredible research
in denial of secure boundaries
aiming for generational joy.

That unbending refrain can only lead to
one transparent conclusion.
Here I stand on scientific findings,
maintaining respiration
while dissenters resist adapting
the greatest good for the greatest number.
In essence, then, I stand alone
in anticipation of that promised
celebration of personal hand-holding,
unrestricted hugs, profound touch.

FLOWER POWER

On my way to shake the pastor's hand on
Mother's Day, a little girl at church
handed me a miniature rose.
Small enough to park above my
kitchen sink, it bloomed there another
two weeks. Then I relegated the plant
to the back porch rail where it stayed
through June into October.

Suddenly a new bud made its presence known.
I brought in the rose, gave it a drink of
warm water, set it beside the purple orchid
on the pine living room windowsill.
One after another, three buds opened, peach in color,
bringing me a smile each morning.
With a fresh, hot cup of coffee, I
postpone the day, watching roses bloom.

VII

Ageism

NINETIETH SUMMER

Lazing on the deck under a blue, blue sky
interspersed with white puffs of cloud,
I laugh at cannibalistic Norway gulls
screeching as they dive to retrieve
discarded bones of drumsticks on the grass—
bird devouring bird.

It had been a challenging walk down the street
to meet with loved ones for this barbecue.
Family time—the highlight of July—
pushed me on, step by step.

High above, a swarm of dragonflies sweeps through
descending greenheads on our behalf.
Conversation swirls around hostas reaching
longed-for growth, only to be destroyed
by an otherwise loved family of deer.
Then, a great-granddaughter's need to have
her chicken cut into tiny bites to accommodate
missing front teeth.
Another loss by favored Mets.
Another dread shooting of innocents.

Lying back, I muse sketched-in plans to fulfill
my ninetieth summer.
Poetry occupies first place in this agenda,
with one assignment for the third Wednesday of the month
completed. Poems have been sent to Painted Poetry III.
Choices must be made for the July reading at the library.

Next, an online course in Ancient Philosophy has begun.
Then, six Thursday mornings at the library to study opera.
Finally, I will attend the Methodist Women's
weekend conference on missions at Georgian Court.
So, July plans are complete.
It is, remember, my ninetieth summer.
August can take care of itself.

THIS HOUSE, MY HOME

The front door stands open wide
where late-day sunshine filters in
to fill yawning space.

When I pour a fresh cup of joe in the kitchen
spicy odors of cinnamon and ginger
fill the air with invitation.

Between the many shiny windows
shelves and shelves of books display
their inviting titles and familiar progeny.

From wall to facing wall
my arms stretch wide
to focus on their agenda.

The basement holds a rec room
for those tempting clouded days
when nothing else will do.

Sometimes I struggle up narrow stairs;
reach that out-of-the-way pinnacle;
ponder the width and breadth of my world.

Ah, but the lonely bed beckons me
when I enter its sanctuary
as twilight reigns.

I USED TO LIE

I used to lie
flat on the new-mown lawn,
stare straight up
into a passing cloud,
watch it shape itself
into a lamb on a hill,
alone,
away from all other
lambs,
away from bending shepherds,
their curving hooks,
long-limbed reach,
territorial claim.

I would stare until my
lingering gaze
was left with nothing
but a shredded
remembrance.

CONCEIT: THE STRAY

You dog, you!
I watched you slip into the room,
tail between your legs,
sliding against the nearest wall
while we chatted as we clinked
our raised glasses and smiled
at each other's innuendoes.
You hesitated but a moment
then bowed your graying locks
against the friendly, open ear of
the neighbor at your elbow.
You think you're everybody's pet
but your tongue hangs down too low
for fond acceptance. Sit, we beg.
Stay.

I have a bone to pick with you.
I recognize that itch you mean to
scratch. This is not the place for that.
Just one quick pat on the back, then
hightail it out of here to bark at
some other cocktail party.

INTO THE TWILIGHT

Gerontologists have called the "oldest old"
one of the fastest-growing age groups
in the country.
Their world gets a little smaller,
its mysteries a little more pressing.

Through backward glances,
pioneers inch ahead into the twilight.
They do the unthinkable: get older.
They find it amazing, living so long,
keep going on.

They insist rewards outweigh
hardships. In spite of the onset of
dementia, recurring bouts of
anxiety, they dare not talk about
not surviving.

For members of a dwindling group,
losses mount but joys abound.
They gush about new music--
by Lady GaGa and Adele.
With trust in the essential goodness

of humanity, they note human acts
move human evolution along the lines
envisioned by the Poet of Eternity.
So begins a New Year for Pioneers
on an alien frontier.

AUTUMN

When days dwindle down
to a cherished few
I inhale the musk of
melancholy,

recall youth in all its
golden dreams,
slipping off my shoulders,
satin and lace.

Summer's breeze,
soft and airy,
promised playful release
from spring's pounding demands.

Now sharp shadows deepen,
coating my vision in
obscurity.
Let dusk settle upon us.

FROM DEEP WITHIN

From deep within
our collective soul
rises a poignant
longing for peace

between friends
between strangers
from here to the Rockies
between blue states and red.

Some swear they long to go
back to the fifties.
Some sigh for a return to
their childhood.

Some believe their
unforgettable BFF
will satisfy their need,
their longing to hold on

to the way things used to be,
beyond a remembered
longing for love.
We hang our longing by its fingertips

on a telephone line
high above the trees of home
stretching beyond our reach
hatless under the sun,

barefaced beneath the moon,
up on our toes as we yearn
toward each other
from deep within.

HOLIDAY

Extinction of peace pelted last New Year's Eve
for which there can be no apology.
Poking at the wound of regret
will not make it better.

In spite of the fear entangled therein,
imagine another outcome.
The gold of healing shimmers,
a gift within our grasp.

Grab hold with me now to
contemplate what might have been.

A TASTE OF MONEY

It happened at the needful age of ten
when the landlady drafted my help to
dust the wooden floor surrounding
the carpet in her living room.
Then, because I was so handy, she
showed me how to polish her end tables.
At the end of the time that took, she
handed me a quarter with a smile.

My mother allowed me to go by myself
all the way up to Main Street, where I
browsed through Grant's Department Store
until I came across a counter full of
dolls' clothes. They really took my eye
since I had gotten a longed-for doll at
my last birthday. Just a little thing,
twelve inches she was, and still in the

same dress she arrived in. My twenty-five
cents went for her first new outfit. How
excited I felt! I couldn't wait to get home
to try it on her. It was perfect!
My future earnings were anticipated with
joy and expectation. The meaning of Work

was sketched on my mind right then and there.
Twenty years down the road found me

looking forward with eagerness to the
next day's promise of well-earned money
to provide another new dress for
another much-loved doll.

SCULPTURE

One shoulder raised in an attitude of
perhaps
she bares her willing
acquiescence
amid the murmurs of the approving
class,
would-be sculptors all.

To capture the essence of
appealing dimples at the
base of her fluid spine,
she stands precisely in
the center of the room,
head thrust back, eyes closed
against the penetrating light.

The wood of wild cherry
resists each probing knife.
Furrowed brows concentrate
agonizing moments
in attempts to capture
the delicate determination
of her willing mouth.

Like a soldier, her arms resist
mobility.

THE WHISTLER

Coaxed from bed, I stumbled
against the open drawer,
floundered just a minute,
landed on the floor.

Lying there, I listened,
heard it once again,
a plaintive tune so lonesome
I longed to take it in

to hold it close for comfort
to still its needy cry
but no matter how I reached
its whistle passed me by.

Stumbled back to bed
to lie awake til dawn,
trembled while the whistle
carried on and on.

Coffee in the morning
calmed me once again
until that lonesome whistle
echoed from the glen.

Slipping on my sneakers
I headed out the door
following its echo
toward the distant shore.

Splashing over water
the whistle trembled near.
I closed my lips to listen.
All at once it's clear.

All the while I followed
it startled me to know
I'm the searching whistler!
my cheeks were puffed to blow.

RETREAT

Since Daylight Savings Time, my bedside clock
Is an hour behind. I let it be. I know the time.
The time is now.
The day is today. The choice is mine.
Whether to lie here a little longer or
Head straight for the shower is my own
First decision of the day. I've come back
From the rat race long traveled to
Commute from home to career,
From struggle to compete in intertwining
Circles of Self, Friendships, Loves, Education,
Parental duties. My children, long grown,
Bless me with their caring ways.
I cast my eyes across the many detours
Lining their journeys,
Remembering my own,
Helpless to shed light on their paths
In this, my dotage.
It's been a long, convoluted trip.

BEYOND ALL SAINTS DAY

On our knees at hint of dawn
We enter November like a prayer.
Pewter smoke curls into mottled grey cloud,
Portender of color-drained days to wrap
Round our descent into isolation.

We dead-head fading chrysanthemum buds,
One last attempt to prolong bloom.
We stare into a sunless sky in search
Of a passing flock. They left so soon we
Cannot recall their last honking goodbye.

Yesterday's apples bobbed in the tub.
Yesterday was but a game. Now green
Peelings curl in one long sweep.
Round and round the Granny Smith
Whirls through practiced fingers.

Days simmer by in soups and stews.
Here in the kitchen we
Don't miss the sun.
We anticipate our brood's return.
Baking warms our waiting.

Time with autumn leaves whipped
By winds into frenzied swirls
Pits against clouded glass.
Winds die down.
Lone evening descends.

Silence intrudes.
Its familiar suit
Waits at the door to interrupt
Willful attempts to recapture bliss.
November breathes one final Amen.

.

READY TO MAKE A NEW BEGINNING

But nothing ever ends.
In the middle of wherever I am,
The past I plot to escape
Will find itself trounced underfoot.
Our lives are woven of many threads,
One strand interwound with another
For strength and permanence.
In today's demands for instant success
No room for failure is tolerated.
A "bride's biscuits" are never experienced
Since perfection is at hand at the corner bakery.

Even the most intimate of marital closeness is
Tried on beforehand. To learn as you go
Induces smug intolerance among peers.
Decades have gone by since anything bridal
Held a bouquet of familiarity for me.
This New Year's Resolution, then, involves no one else,
No one to please, or satisfy, or impress.
Simply put, I plan to reach a deeper self
Beneath casual layers of sensibility
Wrapped around my personhood.
I have an idea it's dark down there.